MYST

OF THE ANCI

GEOGLYPHS

PAUL G. BAHN

WEIDENFELD & NICOLSON
LONDON

N ot content with producing images – paintings, engravings, sculptures or figures pecked into rocks – of modest size, scattered around their environment, prehistoric people sometimes undertook the decoration of hillsides or even

*T*he Uffington White Horse in Oxfordshire.

entire landscapes: a category of figure known as 'geo-glyphs' or ground drawings. They include the most enor-mous images ever produced by our prehistoric ancestors.

Mounds and Sculptures

*A*erial view of the Great Serpent Mound, Ohio.

One kind of geoglyph involves the piling up of earth or sand into mounds to form patterns. The best known are the large prehistoric earthen mounds of the north-eastern USA, some of them built in animal shapes – for example, the Great Serpent Mound of Ohio, dating probably to the final centuries BC, which is almost 390 m long, 6 m wide and 1.5 m high. It has the form of a curved serpent which seems to hold an egg in its jaws.

The Aborigines of Arnhem Land and neighbouring parts of Australia make sand or earth sculptures, during mortuary or healing rites – they include humanlike forms, images of giant fishtraps and so forth; and it is very probable that such ephemeral art forms also existed in prehistory, not only in Australia but also in other parts of the world.

Chalk Figures

Among the most famous geoglyphs in the world are the giant hill figures of Britain, images made by removing turf above chalk to make a bright white line against a green background. These figures require regular scouring to have their whiteness maintained, and to prevent being overgrown. If left untended for more than 20 years, the white lines disappear.

The two great human figures, the 'Long Man of Wilmington' in Sussex, and the very phallic 'Cerne Abbas Giant' in Dorset are of unknown age; however, there is no doubt that the Uffington Horse in Oxfordshire, 110 m long, is prehistoric. Long thought to be of the Iron Age, from comparisons with horse figures in Celtic

Aerial view of the Uffington horse, now known to be a creation of the British Bronze Age.

art, but also ascribed by some to Anglo-Saxon times, it has now been shown, through optical dating (which shows how much time has passed since buried soil was last exposed to sunlight) of silt laid down in the lowest levels of the horse's belly, to date back to the Bronze Age, in the range 1600–1400 BC, about 1,000 years older than previously thought. Some researchers believe the animal is actually a dragon, since the flat hill in the valley below is called Dragon Hill, and there is a legend that St George killed the dragon here, and that the spot where the blood spilled is now a patch where nothing grows.

The 'Long Man of Wilmington', 70 m tall, holds a staff in each hand, and is thought to be Europe's biggest human depiction. Thought by many to be prehistoric – possibly a warrior, or a fertility symbol deprived of genitalia by Victorian prudery – it may also be later, since there are analogies with the stance of a soldier holding two standards (on 4th-century coins)

*D**ragon Hill viewed from the Uffington White Horse; legend has it that the white patch on the hill is where St George killed the dragon.*

and a 7th-century belt buckle from Kent showing a warrior with a spear in each hand, while some ascribe him to medieval times. The earliest recorded evidence of his existence is a drawing from 1710. The figure was restored in 1969, having been camouflaged with green paint during the Second World War to avoid being a landmark for enemy aircraft. A trial section cut across one of the staves showed that the trench cuts through the soil but only about 5 cm into the chalk beneath, and is filled with chalk rubble, whereas the Uffington horse was cut as much as a metre into the rock, and then filled with rubble – the cutting and filling have been done repeatedly since at least 600 BC. The hardness of the trench walls will have guided the scourers' tools, so that the outline will scarcely have varied through time.

The Cerne Abbas Giant is the most enigmatic of the chalk figures. He faces the sunset, and stands 55 m high from the top of his head to the soles of his feet (almost twice as high as the Colossus of Rhodes, one of the Seven Wonders of the Ancient World), and 65 m high from his feet to the top of the knobbly club, 37 m long, which he wields with his right hand. He is naked except for what may be a belt; he has eyebrows, eyes and a mouth, with a long grassy mound for a nose; he has a nipple and three ribs at either side, placed asymmetrically, and what may be his collarbones. Finally, he displays both testicles and an erect phallus, now 7.2 m long. However, his phallus was originally shorter. Until the late 19th century, the giant also had a navel, but when he was scoured in 1908 a mistake was made (probably because this area had become grassed over), and the navel was incorporated into the 4.8 m phallus.

The giant's outline is a neatly edged trench, about 40 cm wide and cut about the same distance into the soil and chalk below – taking the figure's size into account, its original layout involved the digging of about 25 tonnes of chalk from almost half a kilometre of trench, a very significant amount of work.

The Long Man of Wilmington, Sussex.

*T*he chalk-
cut figure
of the Cerne
Abbas Giant,
whose identity
and date remain
subjects of
controversy.

There are still two points of deep disagreement. The first is this figure's date. Since there are no mentions of it before 1694, when parish accounts recorded a bill of three shillings 'for repairing ye giante', some historians ascribe it to that period or shortly before. Others, however, are equally adamant that it is ancient. It is hoped that optical dating, as at Uffington, will soon clarify the issue.

But if it is ancient, what or whom does it represent? Many have seen it as a

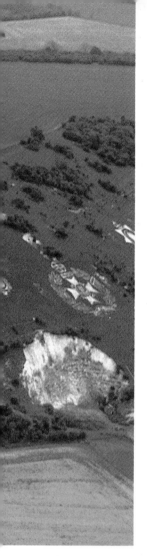

Romano-British depiction of Hercules, brandishing his club, and with a (now disappeared) lion-skin on his outstretched arm. Most recently, however, it has been claimed that the left arm has a cloak dangling from it, and may even have once held a severed human head in its fist. In other words, this would be an Iron Age image of a god, a guardian of the local tribe, the Durotriges.

There were probably many more chalk figures in Britain in prehistoric times, but they have not survived. The others which can be seen are all of very recent age – for example, the Uffington horse seems to have inspired a wave of 18th- and 19th-century white horse carvings across the Wiltshire Downs, seven of which still remain (e.g. at Alton Barnes, Hackpen Hill and Westbury). Yorkshire has the Kilburn Horse, cut in 1857 and whitened with lime; while Scotland has a late 18th-century horse and stag on Mormond Hill, Grampian. In Buckinghamshire, there are huge white crosses at White Leaf Hill and Bledlow Ridge, variously attributed to medieval monks and Cromwell's troops. The practice still continues, such as a crown cut in Kent in 1902 to celebrate the coronation of Edward VII; an aeroplane by Dover castle, cut after Blériot's cross-Channel flight in 1909; a 73 m long kiwi, cut by New Zealand troops on Beacon Hill, near Salisbury Plain, in the First World War; and, largest of all, a 192 m lion cut into the hillside at Whipsnade Wildlife Park, Bedfordshire.

A recent example of hill carving; regimental badges at Fovant, Wiltshire.

*T*he Westbury
White Horse in
Wiltshire is a recent
figure which continues
a prehistoric tradition.

15

Desert Intaglios

The most durable of all geoglyphs are the 'desert intaglios' made in rocky or desert areas by moving aside stones coated with a natural dark varnish to expose the lighter-coloured soil beneath. These exist in Australia, Chile, Arizona and California – in fact about 300 figures of various large sizes are known in the deserts of the American Southwest alone, around the Lower Colorado River – humans, serpents, lizards, mountain lions and apparently abstract and geometric designs. One figure, nicknamed the 'Fisherman', holds a spear, its tip composed of dozens of pieces of white quartz, placed close together.

*A*erial view of two of the Blythe intaglios, California, now fenced to protect them from vehicle tracks and other forms of damage.

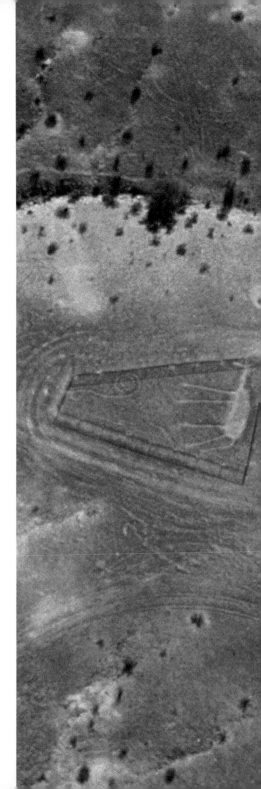

Radiocarbon dating of organic material growing on gravel in figures near Blythe, California, has led to claims that they were created in about AD 890.

To the local Indians, the images are living shrines made by their remote ancestors, but at least one has been used for ceremonial purposes fairly recently, with offerings of feathers, coins and buttons being deposited in small piles of stones around a stick-figure in Arizona. In northern Australia, in historic times, large designs were observed on the surface of the plains. They were made in the dry season, while the ground was still damp, by pounding the

*D*etail of the hand of the human figure at Blythe, showing the simple technique by which it was made, simply by moving aside the darker stones on the surface. earth with stones to make it smooth. These figures, unlike the true desert intaglios, were highly impermanent, but it is probable that they were also made here in prehistoric times.

Geoglyphs are particularly numerous and impressive in South America, notably in Chile and Peru. In northern Chile, for example, over 125 sites are known, with about 2,500 figures; the Tarapacá desert alone has 44 geoglyphs

*G*eoglyphs at Tiliviche, *northern Chile.*

*H*uman figure with a staff, made by piling up earth, and geoglyphs of birds at the site of Altos de Ariquilda I, northern Chile.

which seem to be linked with great temporary campsites and with important caravan routes between oases and between the coastal lowlands and the highland. Some, varying from 5 to 10 metres in size, mostly represent humans with sticks or supports, enclosed in circles, and animals, especially birds. Another group comprise big geometric

*G**eoglyph of a stepped rhombus, at the site of Santa Rosita, northern Chile.***

*G**eoglyphs at Cerros Pintados, Iquique, northern Chile.***

*G*eoglyph of a geometric figure,
about 100 m wide, at Altos de
Ariquilda I, northern Chile.

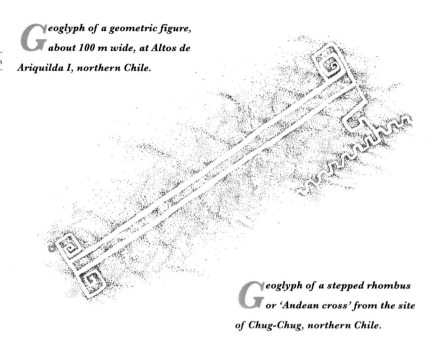

*G*eoglyph of a stepped rhombus
or 'Andean cross' from the site
of Chug-Chug, northern Chile.

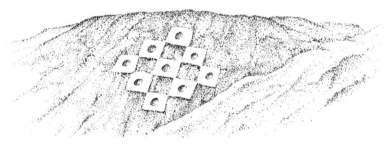

figures (about 100 m long), especially straight lines accompanied by or ending in volutes and meanders.

The site of El Cerro Unita has various straight lines, but also a 100 m anthropomorph with a radiating face, rectangular eyes and mouth, arms bent at the elbows like Vs, and a belt. Santa Rosita has a group of stepped rhombuses. The site of Cerros Pintados has over 350 designs, including schematized humans, men on rafts, big fish and many geometric figures, notably very

*T*he *'Giant of Atacama', at Cerro Unita, near Iquique, northern Chile.* numerous stepped rhombuses, also known as the Andean Cross. Some researchers believe that the latter was an emblem of the Tiwanaku culture (c. AD 600–1000), marking a new area, and integrating it economically and ideologically into the Tiwanaku system and order. The design is certainly tightly linked to caravan routes, and dates back at least to the 4th century AD.

Maria Reiche, the pioneering researcher of the Nasca lines, photographed in Nasca in 1985.

By far the best known examples of geoglyphs, however, are the spectacular and gigantic figures on the plain at Nasca, Peru. Best visible from the air (like most geoglyphs) these images – birds, a monkey, a spider, whales, etc., up to 200 m in size – are found amidst geometric figures such as trapezoids of 3 km, as well as numerous straight lines of as much as 10 km long which some believe

Some of the hundreds of lines that criss-cross the Nasca plain.

*A*erial view of the huge monkey figure on the plain at Nasca, Peru; this is 91 m long.

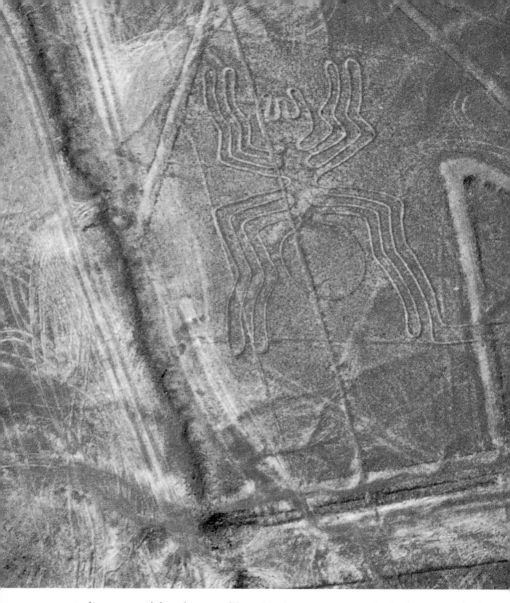

to be ceremonial pathways, although others see a great deal of astronomical involvement in the Nasca layout, with the images perhaps representing constellations. After the dark, well-varnished cobbles were moved aside to make the figures, organic material accumulated on the lighter cobbles beneath and was encapsulated in new rock varnish. Radiocarbon dating of this organic matter

This strange design, dubbed 'ET' is 9 m high and was discovered at Nasca in 1983. It resembles a human foetus with radiating zigzags, and, unusually, was made by piling up material rather than moving it aside.

Aerial view of the great spider figure on the Nasca plain, 45 m long.

has provided results from 190 BC to AD 660, which has been claimed to be a minimum age for the geoglyphs. This is confirmed by the distinct similarities between the animal figures and images on the pottery of the Nasca culture of AD 100-500. The Nasca 'lines' have become most associated with the work of German mathematician Maria Reiche who, from the end of the Second World

War, devoted her life to them, discovering the monkey with its spiral tail, and the spider.

Many of the straight lines radiate out from single points (line centres) which are often low hilltops or ends of ridges – broken pottery found here suggests that religious offerings were made. Many of the lines seem to have served as pathways, probably for religious processions; and most of the animal figures

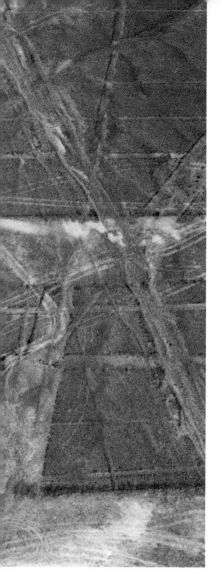

*A*erial view of figures of a 'tree' and a bird, and the metal roadside tower from which travellers on the Pan-American Highway can observe them. Nasca plain, Peru.

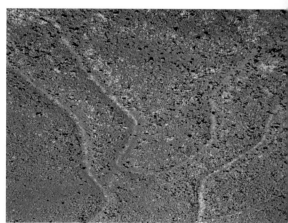

*D*etail of part of the 'tree' figure, Nasca (above), showing how it was made by moving darker surface material aside.

are formed by a single line, so that one can 'enter', walk round the whole design, and 'leave' without crossing or retracing one's steps.

Experiments have shown that the straight lines were very easy to produce, with the simplest of technologies. The great animal figures – like any of the giant figures discussed in this book – were probably drawn in miniature, and then perhaps hugely expanded on to the landscape by means of a simple grid.

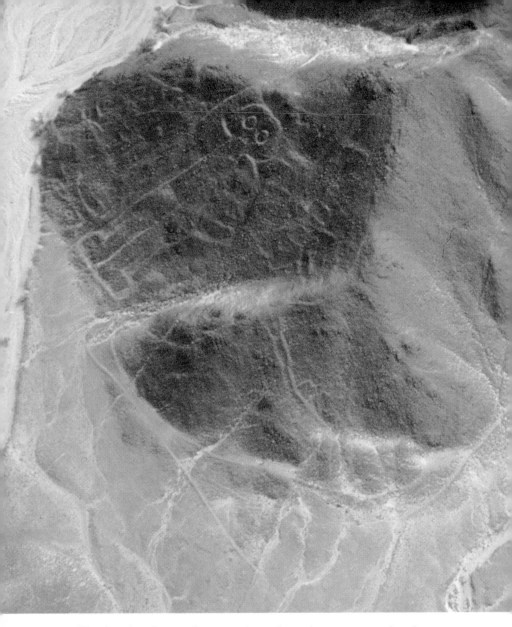

The fact that they are best seen from above does not mean that they ever were in the past (though some have speculated, without any evidence, that the pre-historic Peruvians had the technology to make hot-air balloons). It is far more likely that they were meant to be walked, and/or to be seen by the gods. In the

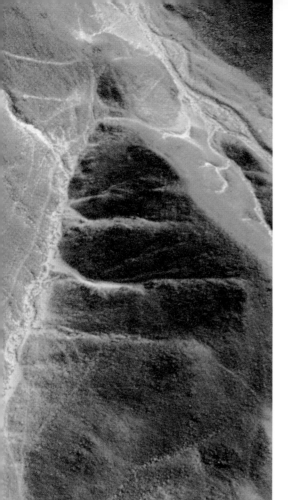

A erial view of the mountainside figure of a waving human, 32 m tall, at Nasca. Maria Reiche calls this the 'Owl-man' and suggests he represents the moon.

same way, the cruciform design of European medieval cathedrals is best appreciated from the sky, but their builders never saw them from that vantage point.

All of the varied geoglyphs in this volume have several things in common. They were produced, with great care and labour, by our ancestors, as truly

monumental images of great religious or symbolic significance. And in some cases they have been deliberately maintained and renewed for centuries. Countless others must have existed, but are now lost for ever. Those which remain are a very fragile and precious legacy, which must be protected. Fortun-

*A*erial view of one of the great hummingbird figures on the Nasca plain.

*A*erial view of another hummingbird design on the Nasca plain (its wingspan is 145 m long).

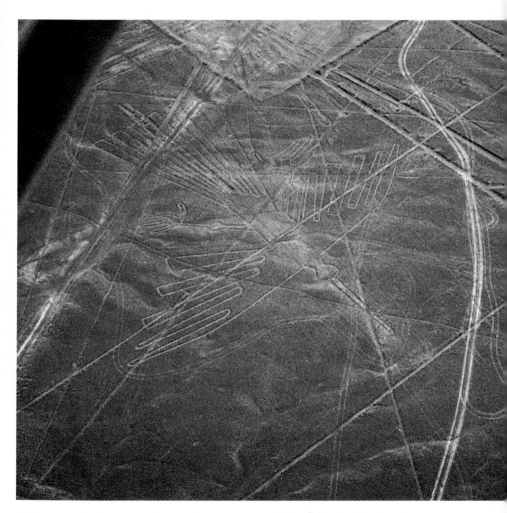

ately, many are in remote deserts, but even some of those (e.g. in the American Southwest) have been deliberately vandalized by people driving motorbikes or jeeps over them. Alas, as can be seen on p. 17, just as the figures were made by simply moving the dark surface layer of stones aside, so tyres have the same

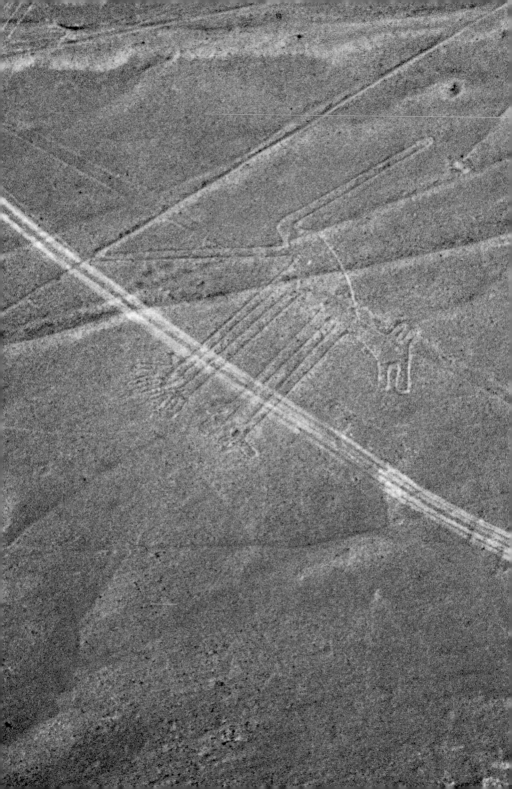

effect, and the tracks and circles left by these vehicles remain as permanent scars next to the images. The only consolation is that geoglyphs are generally so enormous that it would be very difficult to destroy them completely. They are certainly among the most spectacular and impressive images ever produced by human ingenuity, imagination and sheer hard work.

*A**erial view of the 'jackal' figure on the Nasca plain.*

*V**iew of the whale figure on the Nasca plain.*

GEOGLYPHS

PHOTOGRAPHIC ACKNOWLEDGEMENTS
Cover W&N Archives; pp. 2–3 Fortean Picture
Library [FPL]/F.C. Taylor; p 4 Peter Newark's
Western Americana; p. 5 W& N; p. 6 FPL;
p. 8 FPL/F. C. Taylor; p. 10 W&N/Cambridge
University; p. 12 FPL/G.T. Meadows;
pp.13–4 Zefa; pp. 16–7, 18–9 Paul G. Bahn;
pp. 20–21, 22–3, 25 Marc Fasol; pp. 26, 27,
28–9, 30–31, 31tr, 32–3, 33cr, 34-5, 36, 37, 38, 39
Paul G. Bahn.

First published in Great Britain 1997
by George Weidenfeld and Nicolson Ltd
The Orion Publishing Group
5 Upper St Martin's Lane
London WC2H 9EA

Text copyright © Paul G. Bahn, 1997
The moral right of the author has been asserted
Design and layout copyright © George Weidenfeld
and Nicolson Ltd, 1997

All rights reserved. Without limiting the rights
under copyright reserved above, no part of this
publication may be reproduced, stored in or
introduced into a retrieval system, or transmitted,
in any form or by any means (electronic,
mechanical, photocopying, recording, or
otherwise), without the prior written permission
of both the copyright holder and the above
publisher of this book

A CIP catalogue record for this book is available
from the British Library
ISBN 0 297 823167

Picture Research: Joanne King

Design: Harry Green

Typeset in Baskerville